# Sri Lanka Safari

by Grace Hansen

Abdo Kids Jumbo is an Imprint of Abdo Kids
abdobooks.com

abdobooks.com

Published by Abdo Kids, a division of ABDO, P.O. Box 398166, Minneapolis, Minnesota 55439. Copyright © 2025 by Abdo Consulting Group, Inc. International copyrights reserved in all countries. No part of this book may be reproduced in any form without written permission from the publisher. Abdo Kids Jumbo™ is a trademark and logo of Abdo Kids.

Printed in the United States of America, North Mankato, Minnesota.

052024

092024

 THIS BOOK CONTAINS RECYCLED MATERIALS

Photo Credits: Alamy, Getty Images, Minden Pictures, Shutterstock

Production Contributors: Teddy Borth, Jennie Forsberg, Grace Hansen
Design Contributors: Victoria Bates, Candice Keimig

Library of Congress Control Number: 2023948706
Publisher's Cataloging-in-Publication Data

Names: Hansen, Grace, author.

Title: Sri Lanka safari / by Grace Hansen

Description: Minneapolis, Minnesota : Abdo Kids, 2025 | Series: World safaris | Includes online resources and index.

Identifiers: ISBN 9798384900856 (lib. bdg.) | ISBN 9798384901556 (ebook) | ISBN 9798384901907 (Read-to-me eBook)

Subjects: LCSH: Safaris--Juvenile literature. | Natural areas--Juvenile literature. | Sri Lanka--Description and travel--Juvenile literature. | Wilderness areas--Juvenile literature. | Travel--Juvenile literature.

Classification: DDC 954.89--dc23

# Table of Contents

Let's Go on Safari! . . . . . . . . . . . . . 4

Animals of Sri Lanka . . . . . . . . . . . 8

Sri Lanka Experiences . . . . . . . . . 22

Glossary . . . . . . . . . . . . . . . . . . . . . 23

Index . . . . . . . . . . . . . . . . . . . . . . . 24

Abdo Kids Code . . . . . . . . . . . . . . 24

## Let's Go on Safari!

Sri Lanka is an island country in South Asia. It is known for its beautiful and special wildlife. Let's go on safari in Sri Lanka!

A safari is a tour where people can see wild animals in their **habitats**. There are many ways to go on safari in Sri Lanka. Some people go by foot or Jeep. Others go by boat.

## Animals of Sri Lanka

The Sri Lankan leopard is **native** to the country. It is also the top **predator**. Catching a glimpse of one is rare.

Sri Lankan sloth bears are good climbers and swimmers. Females can be seen with their cubs on their backs. Safari-goers are lucky to spot these beautiful animals.

Around 10% of the world's Asian elephants live in Sri Lanka. This makes it easier to **encounter** them. They roam free in open, flat grasslands.

Some people go on a night safari to see certain wildlife. The gray slender loris comes out of its **roost** at sunset.

The yellow-striped chevrotain is also easiest to spot at night. It lives in areas with lots of rainfall. Chevrotains are the smallest hoofed mammals in the world.

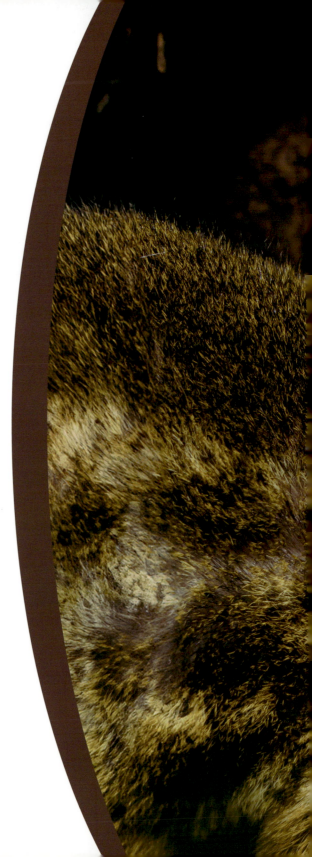

The largest animal in the world can be found off the southern **coast** of Sri Lanka. Blue whales live in the warm ocean waters all year round. They are amazing sights to see!

19

Between January and April, many sea turtles begin to nest in the sand. Some lucky safari-goers can see the **hatchlings**. Others even get the chance to swim with sea turtles!

# Sri Lanka Experiences

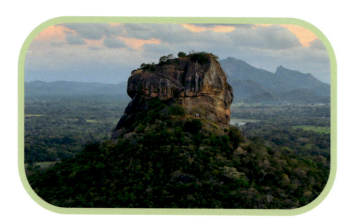

**Climb the Sigiriya Rock Fortress**
Central Province

**Go White-Water Rafting**
Kelani Kanga River

**Tour a Tea Estate**
Nuwara Eliya

**Train Ride with a View**
Nine Arch Bridge

# Glossary

**coast** – the land next to the ocean.

**encounter** – to meet or come upon.

**habitat** – the natural environment of a plant or animal.

**hatchling** – a young animal, such as a bird, reptile, or fish, newly emerged from its egg.

**native** – an animal naturally found in a given place.

**predator** – an animal that hunts other animals for food.

**roost** – a perch on which some animals rest or sleep, or a place containing such perches.

# Index

Asia 4

Asian elephants 12

blue whale 18

gray slender loris 14

Indian Ocean 18

mammals 8, 10, 12, 14, 16, 18

reptiles 20

safari vehicles 6

sea turtle 20

Sri Lankan leopard 8

Sri Lankan sloth bear 10

yellow-striped chevrotain 16

Visit **abdokids.com** to access crafts, games, videos, and more!

Use Abdo Kids code **WSK0856** or scan this QR code!